M000216896

History In Our Attics:

Photos and Documents of Brunswick, Maryland

James R. Castle

Volume I

Published by James R. Castle

October 2014

History In Our Attics:
Photos And Documents of Brunswick, Maryland.

Copyright 2014 by James R. Castle.

All photos and items in this book are from the private collection of James R. Castle. While the physical item depicted is located in the collection, there is a chance copies exist. The author exhaustively researched all items for possible copyright issues. It is the author's belief that no copyright issues exist. Although the author researched all items depicted in this book, he assumes no responsibility for errors, inaccuracies, omissions, or any other inconsistency herein. Any slights are unintentional.

No part of this book may be reproduced or transmitted in any form or by any means, electronic or mechanical, including photocopying, recording or by any information storage or retrieval system without written permission from the author.

James R. Castle
P.O. Box 8
Brunswick, MD 21716

www.Jamesrcastle.com
www.facebook.com/authorjamesrcastle
Follow me on Twitter @Jamesrcastle
Email:Jamesrcastle@comcast.net

Dedication

This book is dedicated to Brunswick's "Greatest Generation". I absorbed as much information as I could and strive to make you proud.

To my wife, who at times must feel second best to a City. Never! You are my motivation.

Ken
Enjoy the Book.

Acknowledgments

This book is not meant to be a "history" of Brunswick. There are other books that serve that purpose. The purpose of this book is to highlight items in the author's personal collection and share his knowledge of those items. The items pictured are not representative of the author's "best" items and future volumes will highlight more from the collection.

Thanks to you, readers, who wish to remember the good times and/or read about those good times.

Thank you to those individuals who assisted me in working out my title and to those that served as beta readers for the book.

Special thanks to Alex Matsuo for her editing skills.

Special thanks to my father, James E. Castle, for discussing railroad logistics and staring at countless photos every day I worked on this book.

Thank you America, where I am allowed to write what I want and able to self-publish, just like Franklin.

About the Author

James R. Castle

James R. Castle was born and raised in the Brunswick/Knoxville area of Frederick County, Maryland. Instead of television or radio, James entertained and educated himself by listening to the stories of his family members and of the elders of his community. Weekends would find James looking for arrow points along a river or digging for bottles from old abandoned dump sites.

James currently resides in Brunswick, MD with his wife, Monica. In his limited free time, James is pursuing a degree from the University of Maryland. He also metal detects, researches, writes and investigates the paranormal. Known as a source on Brunswick area history, James conducts much research on families and properties in the area. He assists the local government with historical research and often contributes to a local weekly newspaper, The Brunswick Citizen.

TABLE OF CONTENTS

Chapter One
The American Civil War

Berlin During The Civil War

Prior to 1890, an area within what we now call downtown Brunswick was called Berlin, which was a small, farming village along the Potomac River.

In 1858, a new, wooden, covered bridge spanned across the Potomac and was held up by eight stone piers. General Robert E. Lee ordered Stonewall Jackson to burn the bridge at Berlin to protect the confederacy. Before sunrise on June 9, 1861, Drake's cavalry drenched the bridge with coal oil and used gunpowder to ignite the bridge. Only the piers remained.[1]

During the Civil War, wherever the Commander for the Army of the Potomac was located, that location was considered to be their headquarters. On two separate occasions, fate would have it that Berlin was used as headquarters. The first following the battle of Antietam in 1862 with Major General George B. McClellan commanding, and the second following the battle of Gettysburg in 1863 with General George G. Meade commanding. Berlin was a logical location for a headquarters because of its easy access to the B&O Railroad and the C&O Canal. During both of these times when headquarters were located here, pontoon bridges were built across the river. A single span crossed the river after Antietam and a double span after Gettysburg. Thousands of troops were camped in Berlin and crossed the Potomac here.

Many do not know the importance of Berlin during the Civil War. These documents show Berlin as an important transportation hub of manpower and supplies during the Civil War.

---

[1] Brunswick:100 Years of Memories, Brunswick History Commission, p175.

(Copy)

Head Quarters. Army of Potomac
Camp near Knoxville Oct 15 1862

Circular.

Division Ordnance Officers are now furnished
with a supply of blank requisitions. Should the
supply fail an ample number to fill up deficien
-cies will always be found at these Head Quarters

These blanks are to be equally distributed
among the several Regiments of their Divisions

They are to be use invariably when on hand, and
if not exact fac-similes will be made in manu-
-script. Every blank must be filled up, — station,
date, Calibre of Arms, — whether smoothbore or rifled
&c — Should any item be omitted, there will be
the only unnecessary delay for which Division Ord.
Officers will be held strictly responsible of sending
back the requisitions for correction —

Every requisition must be approved by the
Commanding Officers of their Divisions and them
-selves, and must be examined carefully and found
unmistakably correct before being furnished to
these Head Quarters — There has been neglect of
duty in this respect heretofore, and it will not
be overlooked hereafter —

By Command of
Major Genl. McClellan
Official — S. Williams

Asst Adjt. General

(Over)

Circular 1862

On the opposite page, handwritten in ink, is a copy of a circular that was drafted in camp at the Headquarters of The Army of the Potomac near Knoxville, MD on October 15, 1862. The circular is by the command of General George McClellan and signed by S. Williams, Assistant Adjutant General, and there was a correction made to William's title. The circular is informing division ordnance officers that blank requisition forms were available and would be distributed among the regiments and further explains the process for filling out the requisitions.

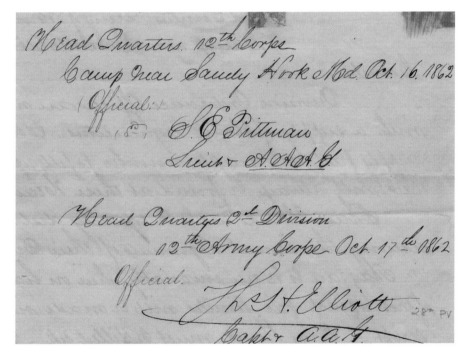

The back of the document states – Headquarters 12th Corps – Camp Near Sandy Hook, MD – October 16, 1862 and signed by S.E. Pittman, Lieut. & Acting Assistant Adjutant General. The document was signed a day later by Capt. Thomas H. Elliott.

Samuel E. Pittman served as an adjutant officer for many years. He is well known for confirming the signature of Lee's Assistant Adjutant General on Lee's lost Special Orders No. 191 found near Frederick, MD.

Captain Thomas H. Elliott was later killed in action at the battle of Peachtree Creek in Georgia in 1864.

No. 40.

SPECIAL REQUISITION.

For *First Brigade Second Div. Cav'y Corps.*

1000	One thousand	Pounds	Blacksmiths' Coal
20	Twenty	Kegs	Horse Shoes
5	Five	"	Mule Shoes
500	Five hundred	Pounds	Horse Shoe Nails
20	Twenty	Setts	Shoeing Tools
1	One		Office Desk & Table

I certify that the above requisition is correct; and that the articles specified are absolutely requisite for the public service, rendered so by the following circumstances: *The former Issue being Expended in Service*

*Wm Knight Lt & A.Q.M.
1st Mass Cav a.q.m
1st Brigade 2d Div*

_____ Quartermaster U. S. Army, will issue the articles specified in the above requisition.

_____ *Commanding.*

RECEIVED at *Berlin Md* the *18* of *July* 186*3*, of *Capt W P Pitkin Asst* Quartermaster U. S. Army, *Two thousand lbs Horse Shoes Five hundred lbs Mule Shoes Five hundred lbs H. S. Nails*

in full of the above requisition.

(SIGNED DUPLICATES.)

*Wm Knight
Lt & R.Q.M 1st Mass Cav
a.q.m 1st Brigade 2d Div*

On the opposite page is a Special Requisition for the 1st Brigade, 2nd Division, Cavalry Corps. Itemized listing includes 1,000 pounds of blacksmith's coal, 20 kegs of horseshoes, mule shoes, 500 pounds of horseshoe nails, shoeing tools, an office desk and a table. The shoeing tools, office desk and table were scratched through and not delivered. These supplies would have been needed following the battle of Gettysburg.

Received at Berlin, MD., the 18th of July 1863, of Capt. P.P. Pitkin, A. Quartermaster, U.S. Army, was 2,000 pounds of horseshoes, 500 pounds of mule shoes and 500 pounds of horse shoe nails.

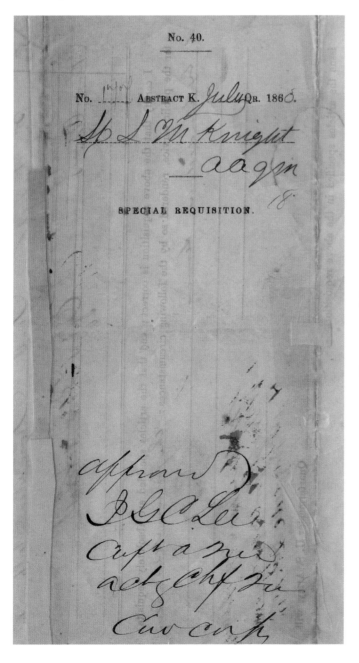

Signed on the reverse by S. M. Knight A.Q.M., and approved by, J.G.C. Lee, Capt., & Acting Chief for Cavalry Corps.

No. 40.

SPECIAL REQUISITION.

For *Use of 2nd Brigade 2nd Cav. Div.*

(13)	Thirteen Setts Wagon Bows	(50)	Fifty Hame Straps
(4)	Four Ridge Poles	(12)	Twelve Tar Pots
(17)	Seventeen Feed Boxes	(3)	Three Spreaders Complete
(4)	Four Tail Gates	(2)	Two Mule Collars
(20)	Twenty Wagon Tongues	(5)	Five Single Whiffle-Trees
(8)	Eight " Covers		
(2)	Two Lead Lines	(3)	Three Kegs Wagon Grease
(8)	Eight Wagon Wheels (Hind)		
(4)	Four " " (Fore)	(12)	Twelve Doz. Open Links
(50)	Fifty Linch Pins		
(20)	Twenty Ring Bolts	(3)	Three Chain Halters
(15)	Fifteen Water Buckets	(20)	Twenty Kegs Horse Shoes ass'd
(1)	One Keg Neats foot Oil	(5)	Five Bags H.S. Nails
(1)	One Doz. Horse Rasps		
(2)	Two Setts Lead Harness	(1500 lbs)	Fifteen Hundred lbs Smiths Coal
(2)	Two " Wheel Do		

I certify that the above requisition is correct; and that the articles specified are absolutely requisite for the public service, rendered so by the following circumstances: *To refit Wagons &c of the Brigade*

Butler Coles
Lt & Regt. Qrmst. Harris Lt Cav
+ A.A.Q.M. 2nd Brigde 2nd Cav Divn

Quartermaster U. S. Army, will issue the articles specified in the above requisition.

_____ Commanding.

RECEIVED at *Berlin Md* the *18* of *July* 186*5,*
of *Capt P P Pitkin* a Quartermaster U. S. Army, *Twenty Kegs Horse Shoes Two hundred & fifty lbs H.S. Nails Three Kegs Grease Fifteen hundred lbs Coal,*
in full of the above requisition.

(SIGNED DUPLICATES.)

Butler Coles
Lt & Regt. Qrmst. Harris Lt Cav
+ A.A.Q.M. 2nd Brigde 2nd Cav Divn

On the opposite page is a special requisition requesting wagon bows, wagon tongues, feed boxes, wagon covers, lead lines, wagon wheels, lynch pins, water buckets, harnesses, tar pots, mule collars, wagon grease, chain halters, horse shoes, horse shoe nails, blacksmith coal, and more.

The items were needed to refit wagons of the brigade after the battle of Gettysburg. The provisions were received at Berlin, MD on July 18, 1863, of Capt. P.P.Pitkin and in full of the above requisition, Butler Coles, Lt. & Regt. Quartermaster, Harris Cavalry Lt. and Assistant Acting Quarter Master.

The reverse is signed by Captain P.P. Pitkin and approved by Capt. J.G.C. Lee and Captain B. Wagoner.

Butler Coles, who twice signed this requisition, served with the 2nd New York Cavalry. He was later captured in the Battle of Thoroughfare Gap, Virginia, on August 14, 1863, and was held as a prisoner of war in Macon, GA. He was paroled on May 14, 1864.

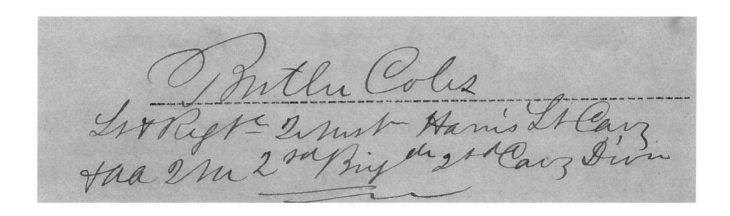

Butler Coles' Signature

No. 27.

LIST OF QUARTERMASTERS STORES, &c., *Rec from Capt P P Pitkin* Quartermaster
U. S. Army, *to Capt Wm Bloodgood aQ't* Quartermaster U. S. Army,
at *Berlin Md*, on the *11* day of *Nov*, 186*2*.

NUMBER OR QUANTITY.	ARTICLES.	COST WHEN NEW.		CONDITION WHEN DELIVERED.	REMARKS.
		Dolls	Cts.		
1 *One*	*Horse*	*Unknown*		*Good*	

I CERTIFY that I have this day *received from Capt P P Pitkin aQ't* Quartermaster U. S.
Army, at *Berlin Md*, the articles specified in the foregoing list.

Wm Bloodgood Capt & aQt Quartermaster.

This "List of Quartermasters Stores" documents the transfer of one horse, in good condition from Captain P.P. Pitkin to Captain William Bloodgood. Both were quartermasters for the Union Army. The horse was transferred on the 11th day of November in 1862. The cost of the horse when new was unknown.

No. 27.

LIST OF QUARTERMASTER'S STORES, &c., *transfer'd* by *Capt. Wm Stoddard Ast* Quartermaster
U. S. Army, to *Capt. P. P. Pitkin* *Ast,* Quartermaster U. S. Army,
at *Berlin Md.* . on the *16th* day of *July* , 186*3*.

NUMBER OR QUANTITY	ARTICLES	COST WHEN NEW.		CONDITION WHEN DELIVERED.	REMARKS.
		Dolls.	Cts.		
128,268	One hundred twenty eight thousand two hundred and sixty eight pounds Oats			Good	
652,256	Six hundred fifty two thousand two hundred and fifty six pounds Mix Grain			"	

I CERTIFY that I have this day *transferred* to *Capt. P. P. Pitkin Ast,* Quartermaster U. S.
Army, at *Berlin Md.* , the articles specified in the foregoing list.

Wm Stoddard
Capt ast Quartermaster.

This "List of Quartermaster's Stores" documents the transfer of supplies by Captain William Stoddard to Captain P. P. Pitkin. Both were Assistant Quartermasters for the Union Army. Transferred on July 16, 1863 at Berlin, MD was 128,268 pounds of oats and 652,256 pounds of mixed grain.

Perley P. Pitkin, was commissioned 1st Lieutenant of the 2nd Vermont Infantry, on June 6, 1861. He was promoted to Captain in the U.S. Quartermaster's Depart. He was promoted to Colonel on August 2, 1864.

Chapter Two

The Baltimore and Ohio Railroad
Brunswick Railroading

The B&O Railroad and the C&O Canal Company both reached Berlin in 1834.[2] The railroad employed a small section gang, and the village was a canal town and relied primarily upon the canal for commerce. That fact changed with the demise of the C&O canal operation and the decision by the B&O to move its main yard operation here from Martinsburg, West Virginia.

Foreseeing a problem with having two Berlins in Maryland (the other on the eastern shore), the name of the town we know today was changed to Brunswick. Old Berlin was slowly demolished and the town moved higher, out of the floodplain. Some of the structures were dismantled and moved. A "boomtown" quickly emerged. The increase in railroad workers and their families demanded housing, stores, churches, organizations, schools, and recreation. Railroading in Brunswick experienced its ups and downs until its demise in the 1970's. All that remains are memories, images and documents of Brunswick's railroading heyday.

B&O Engine and Coal Tender at Brunswick 1913.

---

[2] Brunswick:100 Years of Memories, Brunswick History Commission, p69.

These photographs are circa 1900 and show the ongoing construction of the Brunswick Railroad Yard. More specifically, these photos shows the eastbound "hump". Here, individual trains were "made up" with the help of nature's gravitational pull.

This enlargement of the yard photo shows workers moving track rail. Notice the other details in the photo such as the wheelbarrow, the rail and ties on the flatcar, and the steam shovels.

This enlargement of the yard photo shows an early marked B&O gondola car and a horse and wagon cart.

This enlargement of the yard photo show steam shovels, a work crew and many railroad cars in the yard.

This enlargement of the yard photo shows a track car in the yard. Notice the old abandoned building in the background.

A Dangerous Job

Railroading is a dangerous job. In the cab of a train or in the yard, danger lurks everywhere.

An early train wreck on the line between Brunswick and Knoxville.

A diesel engine derailment on December 31, 1977. The Brunswick Roundhouse is in the background.

Removing diesel from the derailed engine.

Arden Webber (the author's great-uncle) on a B&O Wrecking Crane in Brunswick.

J.L Ayres (the author's great–uncle), Dick Arvin, E.M. Lowell, and Carroll Phillips on a B&O Wrecking Crane in Brunswick.

Both this photo and the photo on the following page show the B&O Wrecking Crane assisting with maintenance of the Brunswick Turntable.

1908 Postcard showing the Brunswick Yards still under construction.

The East Car Yard 1925.

This postcard shows the "New" Brunswick Roundhouse that replaced the "Old" Brunswick Roundhouse in 1907.

A 1908 postcard showing the B&O Shops in Brunswick. Notice the artist outline on some objects.

Support the War Effort!

These ladies stepped up to support their country. During World War I and World War II railroad men were called to military service. But the war effort relied upon the railroads to move soldiers and supplies so, many women stepped in to fill the railroad jobs until the men returned. This picture was taken during World War I. Note how their legs are wrapped so their coveralls do not get caught up in machinery.

Railroad Time Books

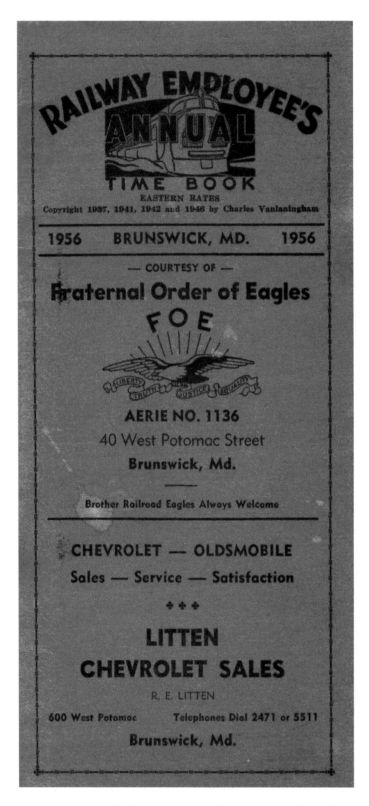

Railroaders kept track of the time they worked in a weekly time book like the one pictured above. This time book is from 1956, and advertises the Brunswick Eagles Club and Litten Chevrolet.

This time book is dated 1945 and was either bought at Horine's Drug Store or the drug store gave it away as a premium.

April a   1945

date	Sun. St	Mon. Rel.	Tue. Hrs	Wed. Min	Thu. Fri. Sat. Foreman	Total Time	Rate per Day	AMOUNT $	Cts.
1	Off – Examined for army								
2									
3	11⁵⁹p	8a	8		Schaumm & Seward			9	06
4	8a	4p	8		J. H. Fleetwood			13	59
5	"	"	"		"			8	54
6	"	"	"		"			8	54
7	"	"	"		A. T. Laciak			8	54
8	"	"	"		"			8	54
9	"	"	"		J. H. Fleetwood			8	54
10	"	"	"		"			8	54
11	"	"	"		"			8	54
12	"	"	"		J. H. Grimm			9	06
13	"	"	"		"			9	06
14	"	"	"		"			9	06
15	"	"	"		"			9	06
								118	67
	Pension 3 1/4 %						—	3	86
								114	81
	War Bonds						—	6	25
								108	56

This page out of a time book shows that the worker was a foreman (supervisor). It shows days and hours worked and at what pay. The book also names the people he worked with. Note the war time date and the fact that this worker was off for two days being examined for the Army. Also, during this time, war bonds were purchased for $6.25.

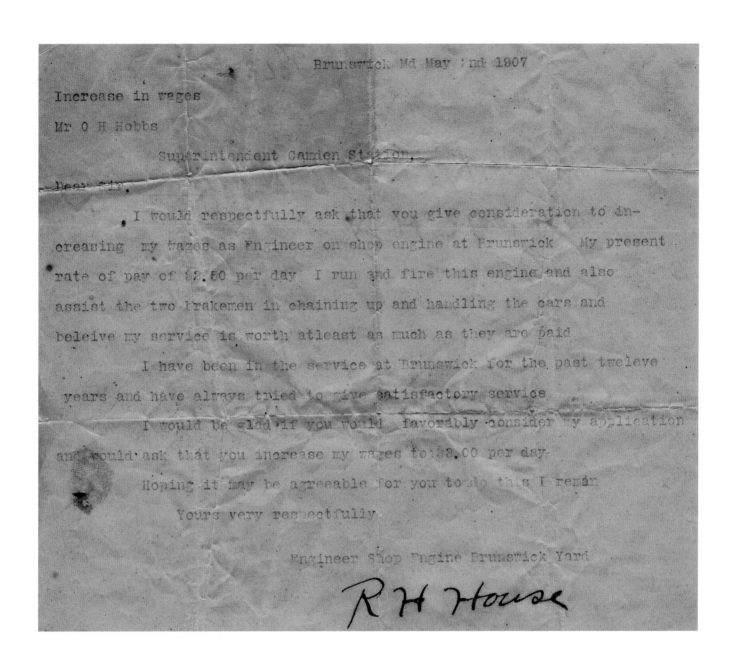

Brunswick Md May 2nd 1907

Increase in wages

Mr O H Hobbs

　　　Superintendent Camden Station

Dear Sir

　　　I would respectfully ask that you give consideration to increasing my wages as Engineer on shop engine at Brunswick　My present rate of pay of $2.50 per day　I run and fire this engine and also assist the two brakemen in chaining up and handling the cars and beleive my service is worth atleast as much as they are paid

　　　I have been in the service at Brunswick for the past tweleve years and have always tried to give satisfactory service

　　　I would be glad if you would　favorably consider my application and would ask that you increase my wages to $3.00 per day

　　　Hoping it may be agreeable for you to do this I remain

　　　Yours very respectfully

　　　Engineer Shop Engine Brunswick Yard

　　　R H House

This letter, faded with time, is a request of R. H .House for an increase in wages for operating an engine at the Brunswick Yard. The letter, in its entirety, is transcribed on the following page.

Brunswick,MD May 2nd 1907

Increase in wages

Mr. O H Hobbs

Superintendent Camden Station.

Dear Sir,

I would respectfully ask that you give consideration to increasing my wages as Engineer on shop engine at Brunswick. My present rate of pay of $2.50 per day I run and fire this engine and also assist the two brakemen in chaining up and handling the cars and believe my service is worth at least as much as they are paid.

I have been in the service at Brunswick for the past twelve years and have always tried to give satisfactory service.

I would be glad if you would favorably consider my application and would ask that you increase my wages to $3.00 per day.

Hoping it may be agreeable for you to do this I remain

Yours very respectfully

Engineer Shop Engine Brunswick Yard

R H House

Join The Union!

Railroad craft unions representing workers were organized in the 1860's. Railroad unions were some of the strongest unions in the nation. A railroad strike would cause significant delay in transporting needed goods across the country. Numerous unions existed including The Brotherhood of Railway Carmen, The Brotherhood of Railway Trainmen, The Brotherhood of Locomotive Engineers, The Brotherhood of Maintenance of Way Employees, and The International Brotherhood of Firemen and Oilers. At the time these unions were formed, working conditions for railroaders included low pay and dangerous work. These factors were the reason why the unions were formed. Over the years, unions combined forming larger unions such as the United Transportation Union.[3]

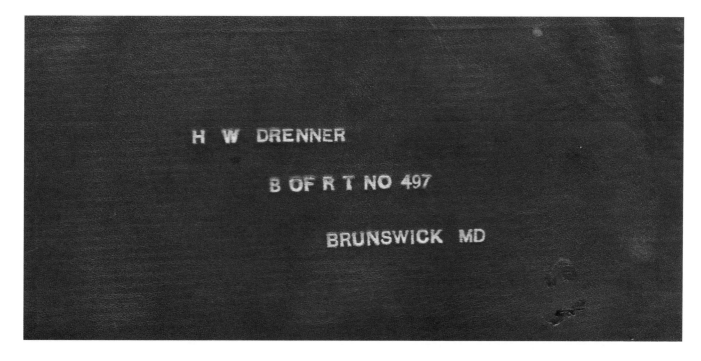

Pictured above is a leather wallet that belonged to H.W. Drenner, member of The Brotherhood of Railroad Trainmen, Number 497, Brunswick,MD.

---

[3] United Transportation Union, Chairman's Manual. www.utu.org

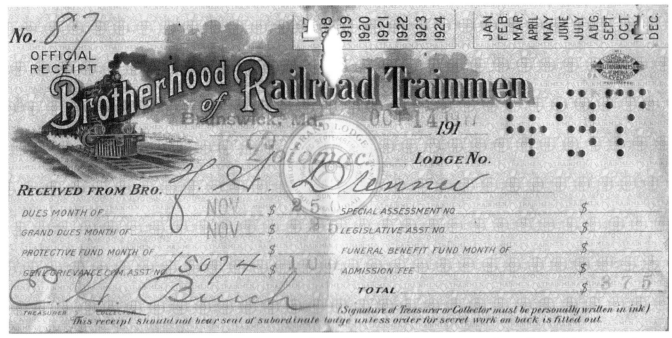

Pictured above is Mr. Drenner's union dues receipt for November of 1917. His monthly dues were $3.75.

Late 1960's / Early 1970's Dodge truck fitted with track wheels.

Men At Work

Side of building marked "Help Save Coal Do Not Make Black Smoke It Wastes Fuel".

This photo shows the last passenger train between Brunswick & Hagerstown on November 1, 1949. Pictured are Earl Kelly, Agent, M.L. Hollar Engineer, & Hagerstown Mayor H.L. Mills.

Chapter Three

The Brunswick B&O Young Mens Christian Association

The YMCA

This 1910 photo shows a cultivated area at the front of the Brunswick YMCA. The front of the building faced the railroad. This photo shows both the YMCA and the hospital annex connected with a walkway. Standing by the fountain is Brunswick Yardmaster Jonathan Martin.

The Brunswick YMCA

No other building in the history of Brunswick had more connection to the community than the Brunswick YMCA. Opened in 1907, the "Y" provided train crews a place to eat, sleep and relax. The unique feature of the building was its inclusion of the community. The building had a restaurant, meeting rooms, a chapel, a barber shop, a bowling alley, and much more.

The Y's influence was greater than just a building on East Potomac Street. An athletic field, later to be named Scheer Stadium, after B&O General Manager E. W. Scheer, was the best athletic stadium in the area. The YMCA also managed the Brunswick Swimming Pool.

A devastating fire destroyed the YMCA in 1980. The lot remains a vacant green space, Railroad View Park, to this day. All we have left are memories, photos, documents and items from the Brunswick YMCA.

The "Y"
and How

BRUNSWICK Y.M.C.A.

A Picture Story of Progress
of the equipment, finances and general
activities of the Brunswick Y. M. C. A.
What has been done to improve the service
to the Member and the Prospective Member.

This promotional booklet was published by the Brunswick YMCA in 1929.

This is a picture of Harvey Bickel, the YMCA General Secretary, from the promotional booklet "The Y and How". The General Secretary, also sometimes called the Secretary, managed the operations of the local YMCA. Bickel was instrumental in the construction of Scheer Stadium, organizing swimming in Catoctin Creek, and organizing excursion trips for Brunswick Youth.

The next series of photos are from the 1929 "The Y and How" promotional booklet.

H. S. BICKEL
General Secretary

E. William Scheer was the General Manager of the Eastern Region of the B&O Railroad. Harvey Bickel influenced Scheer to develop railroad property into what would be called E. W. Scheer Stadium, or locally called Scheer Stadium, the best athletic stadium in the area.

The Trap-Shooting Stations and Trap-House at the top of the hill at E. W. Scheer Stadium.

This picture shows the trap shooting area that was located at Scheer Stadium.

Lobby of Y.M.C.A. on main floor.

This picture shows the lobby of the YMCA, which was known for providing chairs for railroad men, current and retired, to relax.

This photo shows the laundry room of the Brunswick YMCA along with two workers.

The YMCA Barber Shop.

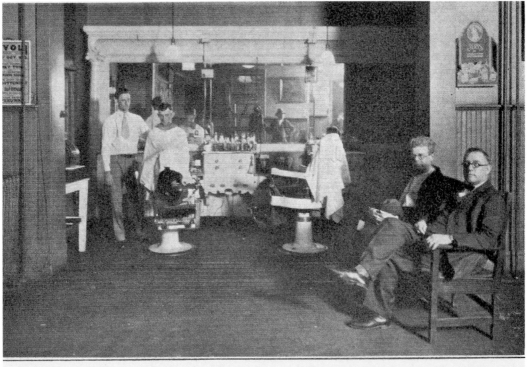

Barber Shop off the lobby.

Bowling Alleys in basement of Y.M.C.A. Building.

This photo shows the two lane bowling alley that was located in the basement of the YMCA.

Dining and Lunch Room.

This photo shows the dining room at the YMCA.

David Emanual Holland was a long time custodian at the Brunswick YMCA. Pictured is his sterling silver key tag from 1918.

A side view of the Brunswick YMCA.

Happy New Year – 1948
Lets see what was on the menu!

M E M B E R S'

SPECIAL NEW YEAR'S DAY DINNER
(Served 11 am   to   11 pm)

$1.00

Celery   o r   Pickles

****

Cream of Tomato Soup or Mixed Fruit Cocktail

****

Choice of,-
Roast Maryland Turkey with Dressing and
Cranberry Jelly or
Roast Sirloin of Beef, Brown Gravy or
Fried Pork Chops (Cooked to order)

Choice of Two Vegetables
Whipped Potatoes   Sweet Potatoes
Creamed Green Peas
Lima Beans   Sauer Kraut
Apple Salad

Choice of Dessert

Ice Cream
Pumpkin Pie   Hot Mince Pie
Peaches in Syrup

Tea   Coffee   Milk

Bread and Butter

"Today's" special New Year's Day Dinner started off with your choice of celery or pickles. Then a choice of cream of tomato soup or mixed fruit cocktail. For the main entree, you had a choice of roast Maryland turkey with dressing and cranberry jelly or roast sirloin of beef, brown gravy or fried pork chops. Next was a choice of two vegetables and then your choice of dessert. Your meal came with a drink and bread with butter. The meal cost $1.00 for members and $1.10 for non-members.

New Year's Day   M E N U   January 1, 1948

Soup 15¢   Fruit Cocktail 15¢
    Celery 15¢   Chow Chow Pickles 10¢

DINNER

(Includes Entree, choice of two Vegetables,
Bread & Butter and Beverage).

Fried Oysters: Small Fry 60¢;   Large Fry 80¢
Roast Maryland Turkey with Dressing and
          Cranberry Jelly . . . . 80¢
Roast Sirloin of Beef, Brown Gravy . . . 60¢
Fried Pork Chops (Cooked to order) . . . 65¢

Choice of Two Vegetables

Whipped Potatoes 10¢   Sweet Potatoes 10¢
    Creamed Green Peas 10¢
Lima Beans 10¢   Sauer Kraut 10¢
    Apple Salad 10¢

DESSERT

Ice Cream 12¢
Pumpkin Pie 10¢   Hot Mince Pie 10¢
    Peaches in Syrup 15¢

Bread and Butter 5¢
Tea 5¢   Coffee 5¢
    Individual bottle Milk 8¢

A LA CARTE

Fried Oysters: Small Fry 35¢   Large Fry   55¢
Roast Maryland Turkey,
    Dressing & Cranberry Jelly . . . . . . 55¢
Roast Sirloin of Beef, Brown Gravy . . . . . 35¢
Fried Pork Chops (Cooked to order) . . . . . 40¢

SANDWICHES

Roast Turkey, with Gravy . . . . 40¢
Roast Beef. with Gravy . . . . 30¢

If you ordered a la carte, the large fry of oysters would cost you 55 cents. A hot turkey sandwich, with gravy cost 40 cents. The food was good and the restaurant busy.

The Swimming Pool

Brunswick Swimming Pool in 1949. The author's great–great grandfather was a boss with WPA when the pool was built in the early 1940's. The pool was part of Scheer Stadium and later turned over to the Town. The pool and bathhouse is still in use today.

You can do it!

Pay Your Dues

The YMCA earned income from selling dues. Pictured below is YMCA Secretary Marvin E. Younkins welcoming a railroader to the "Y". This photo was used as publicity for a membership campaign.

BALTIMORE AND OHIO

RAILROAD DEPARTMENT

YOUNG MEN'S CHRISTIAN ASSOCIATION

BRUNSWICK, MARYLAND

MR. *Dr. Levin West*

IS ENTITLED TO PRIVILEGES AS INDICATED ON THE BACK

RENEWABLE OCTOBER 31, 1932

ANNUAL FEE NOT LESS THAN $5.00

H S Bickel

GENERAL SECRETARY

No. 694

INTERCHANGEABLE MEMBERSHIP TICKET

This is Dr. Levin West's YMCA membership card from 1931. He was issued membership card number 694. Dr. West was born in Petersville, MD and graduated from the University of Maryland Medical School in 1886 and was a surgeon for the B&O hospital. He also served on the Board of Directors of the YMCA. Dr. West volunteered for medical service during World War I. Dr. West was very active in the community and also served as a Town Councilman.[4]

[4] Brunswick:100 Years of Memories, Brunswick History Commission, p195

Evelyn Webber Darr

Evelyn Webber was born in 1916 and raised in Knoxville, MD. She was the daughter of Robert Ashby Webber, a paymaster for the B&O Railroad at Brunswick. She graduated from Brunswick High School in 1933. She later married Sam Darr, a railroader. Sometime after graduation she found employment at the Brunswick YMCA. What started as simple job as a cashier turned into a 45 year career that would last until her retirement in 1981. Evelyn worked her way up into the front office of the YMCA and at one time was the acting General Secretary and held the position of Assistant Director when she retired. Evelyn was the author's great aunt.

This is Evelyn Webber's paycheck from the YMCA issued March 16, 1950. For two weeks work, she was paid $54.91. The check is drawn upon the Bank of Brunswick and is signed by Marvin E. Younkins, Brunswick YMCA Secretary.

A lighter moment in the YMCA office circa 1950. Pictured is Marvin Younkins, Evelyn Darr, Mabel Grey, and Tressa Thompson.

Evelyn Darr and YMCA Secretary Sam Cole in 1964.

Behind the counter at the YMCA is Marvin Younkins, Margaret Moler, and Evelyn Darr in the mid 1950's.

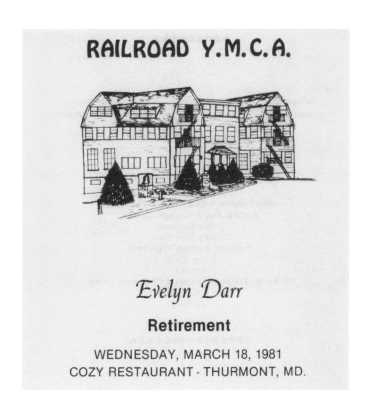

RAILROAD Y.M.C.A.

Evelyn Darr

Retirement

WEDNESDAY, MARCH 18, 1981
COZY RESTAURANT - THURMONT, MD.

The cover of Evelyn Darr's retirement program.

A Gathering Place

Well known as a gathering place in the community, the Brunswick YMCA offered a social setting for folks to get the "news". The barbershop provided a place to talk about baseball while the front porch sitters remembered the old railroad ways and discussed changes in the industry.

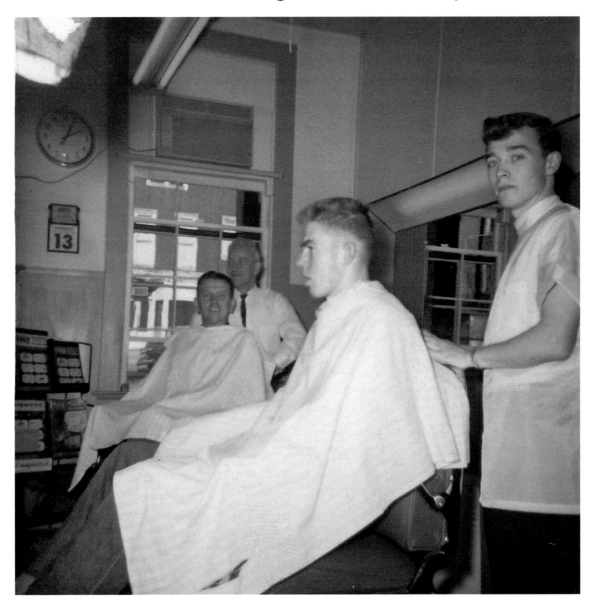

The YMCA Barber Shop in the early 1960's. Pictured is George Merriman and Larry Bussard, barbers and Burgess Porter and Gary Greenfield, customers. Gary Greenfield was the author's father-in-law.

November 8, 1980

Operations were normal on November 8, 1980 until nightfall. Sometime that night , an electrical short in the first floor office and lobby created a fire that destroyed the structure.

A temporary office was opened on Potomac Street during the search for a new location for the YMCA. Numerous locations were considered including rebuilding on the old lot. It took over five years to locate a new site and to construct the new YMCA on Souder Road. The new building was never able to recapture the love of the community like the old YMCA.

The Brunswick YMCA in 1980.

Fire damage to the Brunswick YMCA.

Fire damage to the Brunswick YMCA.

Fire damage to the Brunswick YMCA.

Brunswick YMCA Secretary Glenn Moler attempting to open the safe on the morning after the fire.

RAILROAD Y.M.C.A.
116 EAST POTOMAC STREET
BRUNSWICK, MARYLAND 21716
nov 8 - 1980

An envelope someone took for a souvenir of the Brunswick YMCA.

A Temporary Location

Richard Magalis, YMCA Board Member and Evelyn Darr, Assistant Director, looking out a decorated window on Potomac Street.

Richard Magalis, and YMCA Secretary Glenn Moler at the temporary YMCA Office on Potomac Street.

A New Home

After five years, a new location was selected on the site of the old bowling alley on Souder Road. The new $3.7 million building was dedicated on June 27, 1986.[5] Today, there is no YMCA in Brunswick and the building was demolished in 2014 to make way for a new diner and Inn.

The view of the new YMCA from Souder Road in 1986.

The new YMCA sign visible from Souder Road in 1986.

---

[5] Brunswick:100 Years of Memories, Brunswick History Commission, p145

BRUNSWICK YMCA
Dedication
11:00 A.M.
Friday, June 27, 1986
Brunswick, Maryland

The program cover for the dedication of the new YMCA on June 27, 1986.

Brunswick YMCA Secretary Glenn Moler accepting the new building.

The cake served at the dedication of the new YMCA.

Retired Assistant Director Evelyn Darr and waitress Yonnie
Longerbeam at the reception for the new YMCA.

Chapter Four

Brunswick Stores and Businesses

The Heart of the Community

At the heart of any community are businesses that provide goods and services. In its infancy as a farming village, Berlin required a flouring mill. Production at the mill flourished with the arrival of the B&O Railroad and the C&O Canal. As the population grew, so did the demand for general goods, doctors, pharmacists, etc. When the population "boom" began in 1890, business demands expanded to groceries, hardware, meats, drugstores, and recreational type businesses.

It should be noted that employment with the railroad dictated that employees remained sober. The B&O had no tolerance for intoxicated workers. There were no beer or liquor establishments in Brunswick from the 1890's until the repeal of Prohibition in 1933. Temptation for alcohol was located just two miles away in Knoxville, and many railroaders visited the tiny village known for its many liquor establishments and hotel.

Streets were dirt and certainly muddy when it rained. Wooden plank boards were placed in front of the businesses and some ads touted that they were located on the "Boardwalk in Brunswick". Later, streets were paved and brick sidewalks were constructed. The sidewalk system allowed town residents to exit their house and walk to the "heart" of Brunswick, its downtown. Later expansion of the Town created business locations outside of downtown.

Brunswick's "Circular Economy" was a strong one. In 1957, the railroad was in decline and the annual B&O Railroad payroll in Brunswick was $6 million[6]. Most of that money was earned, spent, deposited, and re-invested, all in Brunswick.

Over the years, business names became synonymous with Brunswick. Stores such as Gross' Store, Kaplon's Department Store, Darr's Confectionary, and Horine's Drug Store were once thought to be able to last forever. Countless other businesses came and went and one by one, as the railroad declined, so did Brunswick's greatest businesses. Frederick, MD and Charles Town, WV became destinations for shopping. Today, downtown Brunswick struggles to retain businesses. All we have left is an exciting new group of businesses and photos, documents, and items that remind us of our favorite Brunswick Businesses from the past.

Go To GROVE'S
ON THE BOARDWALK,
—FOR—
FIRST-CLASS CONFECTIONS
Ice Cream and Soda Water,
Crushed Fruit Sundaes, Soft
Drinks of all kinds.
Opposite Y. M. C. A, Building.

1910 Advertisement for Grove's "On the Boardwalk".

6 Brunswick:100 Years of Memories, Brunswick History Commission, p48

The Brunswick Mill

A mill in Berlin was one of the earliest business in the area and was important for the farming village located here. An entire book should be written just on the subject of Brunswick's mills. Names associated with Berlin/Brunswick mills include C.F. Wenner, John L. Jordan, Graham, and B.P. Crampton. Brunswick's transition into a railroad town and the C&O Canal's demise help lead to a decline in need for a milling operation here. The Brunswick Cooperative began in 1926 in the old mill building and moved to Souder Road in 1962. The old mill building, located near the canal, burned in 1972.

Pictured is an 1886 receipt from Jordan, Crampton & Company to Michael Everhart for a little over 87 bushels of grain.

B. P. Crampton Mill and Grain Elevator circa 1900.

1902 Advertisement for B.P. Crampton & Co. The ad promoted two flour brands, Cream Patent and Excelsior. The ad touts B.P. Crampton & Co as "the leading flour mills of the county" and when referring to their flour, "there is none better".

The Leading Flour Mills of the County.

HIGH GRADE BRANDS
CREAM PATENT
...AND...
EXCELSIOR FLOURS.

MANUFACTURED BY

B. P. CRAMPTON & CO.,
Brunswick - - Maryland.

The above Celebrated Flours are known all over the county and considered the best on the Market. Don't fail to try them. You will want no other. Ask your Grocer for Cream Patent or Excelsior. Remember, there is none better.

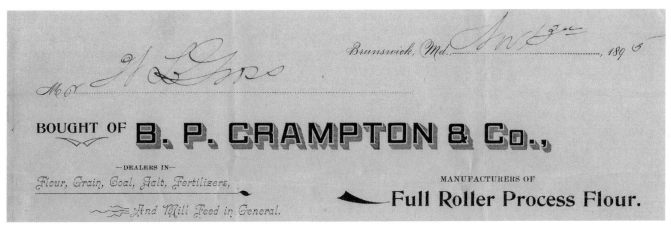

An 1895 billhead from P.B. Crampton & CO for items purchased by Mr. Gross.

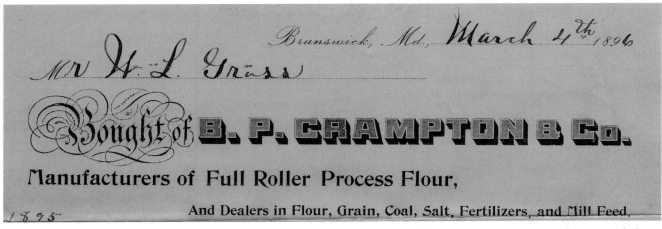

An 1896 billhead from B. P. Crampton for items purchased by Mr. Gross.

H. D. CRAMPTON, President
G. THOMAS DUNLOP, Vice-President

G. H. HOGAN, Secretary
L. E. McBRIDE, Treasurer

Brunswick, Md.,_____ 191___

M_____

TO B. P. CRAMPTON & CO., Inc. DR.

MERCHANT MILLERS
FLOUR, FEED AND MEAL

DEALERS IN GRAIN, ANTHRACITE AND BITUMINOUS COAL, SALT, HAY, &C.

TERMS: STRICTLY CASH
ROBINSON CODE

To prevent Confusion, Sacks charged in this Bill must be paid for. If returned in good order, Money Refunded. Freight on Sacks returned must be prepaid

This is a billhead from B.P. Crampton & Co from the teens.

INCORPORATED UNDER THE LAWS OF THE STATE OF MARYLAND

Brunswick Co-operative Association, Inc. of Frederick County, Maryland

Class B Preferred Stock
$50,000

This is to Certify, That _Wm B Wenner_

is the owner of _Two_ Shares of the Class B Preferred Stock of the "BRUNSWICK CO-OPERATIVE ASSOCIATION, INCORPORATED, OF FREDERICK COUNTY, MARYLAND," transferable only on the books of the Association by the said owner, in person or by duly authorized attorney, upon surrender of this certificate properly endorsed.

The Class B Preferred Stock represented by this Certificate is entitled to an annual dividend of six per cent (6%) payable out of the net profits of the Association before any dividend is paid upon the Common Stock, and in no event shall dividends be cumulative.

The said Preferred Stock is subject to redemption at the option of the Association at any time after April 1, 1931, upon the payment of the par value thereof, or at its book value should its par value be less than its book balue. The said Preferred Stock shall not be entitled to vote at stockholders meetings of the Association except upon the question of mortgaging or placing of a specific lien upon the whole or any part of the property of the Association, and shall not participate in the profits beyond the fixed preferential annual dividend of six per cent (6%).

In Witness Whereof the duly authorized officers of this Association have hereunto subscribed their names and caused the corporate seal to be hereto affixed this _1st_ day of _Sept_ , 1926.

James H Smith
Secretary.

John A Snider
President.

SHARES _two_ EACH

©GOES 178

In 1926, the Brunswick Co-operative Association sold $50,000 worth of Class B preferred stock. This stock certificate shows William B. Wenner purchasing two shares valued at $100 each share on September 1, 1926.

An early booklet containing the Articles of Incorporation and By-Laws of the Brunswick Cooperative Association in Brunswick.

This pin up advertising mirror was given as a Christmas gift to customers of the Brunswick Cooperative Association in the 1940's.

Early Businesses In Brunswick

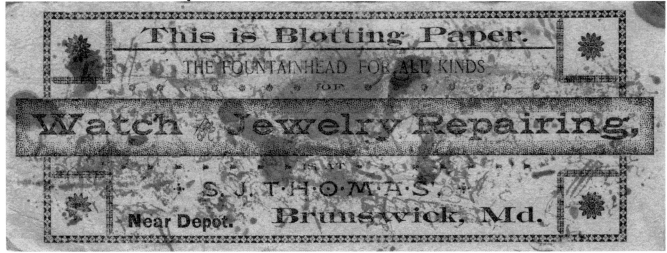

This ink blotter is from S. J. Thomas who had a Jewelry Repair store near the railroad depot in the early 1900's.

Charles Gregory was an early Baker in Brunswick. His bakery, Potomac Bakery, was located on East Potomac Street, which is now an empty lot. On January 14, 1904, while Gregory was making home deliveries, he posed for this photograph.

Jacobs & Ephraim operated a mens clothing store located at 24 West Potomac Street around 1909. This is an advertising shoe horn from the store.

H.N Werntz operated a store on East Potomac Street where today, the Community Garden is located. Beginning as a grocery and dry goods store, clothing was later added. Pictured is an advertising pocket knife for Red Goose Shoes available at H.N. Werntz in Brunswick, MD.

For about eight years during the 1920's, two greek brothers named George and Bill Magoulis operated the Brunswick Candy Kitchen. The brothers made all of the candy they sold by hand. Upon closing the store, the brothers returned to Greece.[7]

This rare token is less than one inch in diameter. The token was valued at ten cents. The token advertised soda, ice cream, and home made candy.

[7] Brunswick:100 Years of Memories, Brunswick History Commission, p107

PHONE 26
BRUNSWICK FRUIT SUPPLY
S. CINCOTTA & SON
FANCY FRUITS AND PRODUCE

Brunswick, Md., ... *192....*

M ....

Address ....

1			
2			
3			
4			
5			
6			
7			
8			
9			
10			
11			
12			
13			
14			
15			

2

Sam Cincotta started his business using a temporary produce stand. He trucked fresh produce from Baltimore to Brunswick. His business was successful and he built the Cincotta Building on West Potomac Street. Pictured is a store receipt for the Brunswick Fruit Supply from the 1920's.

L.B. Darr

Almost one year after the incorporation of the town in 1890, the first set of twins were born in Brunswick. The happy parents named their twins Luther Brunswick Darr and Lula Brunswick Darr.

Luther, or "Lute" as most of Brunswick knew him, was active within the community and owned and operated a confectionery and luncheonette.

Darr's Confectionary was located at 5 East Potomac Street, now part of Square Corner Park. The business opened in 1915 and offered patrons good food, a soda fountain, ice cream, candy, tobacco, and in later years, "the coldest beer in town". Lute operated the business for 47 years before retiring in 1961. Darr's Tavern continued to operate there for many years.

L. B. DARR

The Big Confectionery Store

SODA - ICE CREAM

Headley's Chocolates Fresh From Factory

Cigars :-: Cigarettes :-: Tobacco

SERVICE - COURTESY

BRUNSWICK - - - - MARYLAND

LUTHER B. DARR

"A Good Place to Eat"

JUST AROUND THE CORNER

Soda   Ice Cream   Candy

Cigars   Cigarettes   Tobacco

BRUNSWICK, MARYLAND

SERVICE   COURTESY   QUALITY

Pictured is a business card from L.B. Darr's "A Good Place to Eat" "Just Around The Corner". Specializing in service, courtesy, and quality.

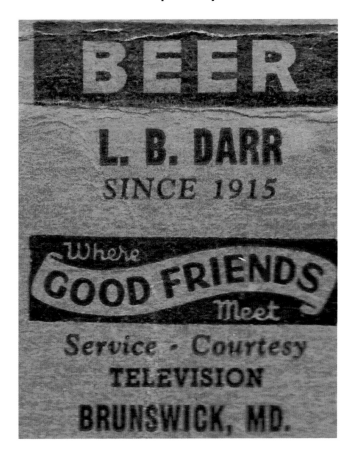

A 1950's matchbook from L.B. Darr.

Distances From Darr's Luncheonette

Baltimore	60
Boonsboro	29
Braddock	19
Chambersburg	53
Charles Town	14
Cumberland	100
Emmittsburg	37
Ellicott City	50
Frederick	14
Gaithersburg	36
Gettysburg	49
Hagerstown	32
Harrisburg	86
Hancock	58
Harpers Ferry	7
Knoxville	3
Lancaster	101
Martinsburg	27
Middletown	12
Ridgeville	28
Rockville	50
Thurmont	30
Union Bridge	34
Washington	66 and 55
Winchester	39
York	78

How far would you drive for good food?

Slot machine tokens from L.B. Darr's

No. 673

BRUNSWICK, MD. February 10 1953 65-232/521

PAY TO THE ORDER OF J. R. Beck $19.95

Nineteen 95/100 _____ DOLLARS

FOR _____

To THE BANK OF BRUNSWICK
BRUNSWICK, MD.   William B. Gross

J. R. BECK
WALL PAPER
BRUNSWICK, MARYLAND

BRUNSWICK, MD.
JUN 2
9 - PM
1952

Mr. William Gross.

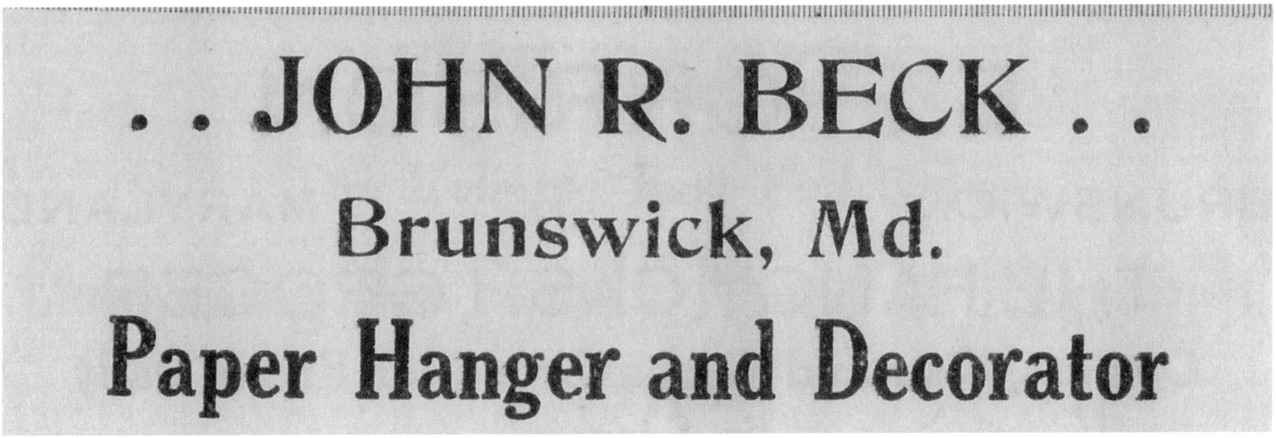

. . JOHN R. BECK . .

Brunswick, Md.

Paper Hanger and Decorator

John Ray Beck was a wallpaper hanger and decorator operating
from the 1920's into the 1950's.

Brunswick had many cab and taxi services over the years including Chick's Taxi, which operated during the late 1940's and 1950's. Pictured is an advertising matchbook for Chick's Taxi.

THE IMPERIAL

PROGRAM

FOR

Week of November 13th to 18th, '16

Published Weekly

Keep this for your ..Daily Reference..

.....PRICES.....

Adults . . . . . 10¢

Children (under 12) 5¢

Unless otherwise advertised

THE RINKER PRESS

The Imperial Theater provided 50 years of entertainment in Brunswick. It was located on West Potomac Street across from the old firehall. Today, an empty lot sits instead. In 1916, the cost of admittance was ten cents for adults and a nickel for children under twelve. In 1916, the movie theater showed two movies a day, some starting with a continuation of a series. The highlight of this week was Poisoned Lips directed by and starring Francis Ford.

1923 ad for the Brunswick Garage.

WILLYS-KNIGHT $1350 DELIVERED

Brunswick Garage

PHONE 172

OVERLAND, $595 DELIVERED

Chapter Five:
Brunswick Organizations
Socializing While Giving Back To The Community

Many residents of Brunswick belonged to organizations. Membership in these organizations was a way to give back to, and improve, the community. There were arts organizations, fire and rescue, business groups, the Lions Club, Masonic organizations, youth oriented groups, and clubs like the Moose and the Eagles. Today, Brunswick is known for its community spirit, taking care of each other, and volunteering to make the community a better place.

The By-Laws and Rules of Order of the Knights of Pythias Brunswick, MD. The booklet is dated 1917.

The Brunswick Red Men
Delaware Tribe Number 43

Delaware Tribe Number 43 was organized as a fraternal organization on July 5, 1867 and operated for 78 years. In 1873, the tribe purchased a building that became the Town's first Red Men's Hall. In 1904, a new building was dedicated that later housed the Eagles Club and now, the Brunswick Heritage Museum. Not only did the Red Men use the building for their purposes but the building became the focal point of the community for social events and entertainment. By 1906, membership reached 380.

The first Red Men's Hall located at the foot of what is now South Virginia Avenue.

The Brunswick Red Men's Hall on what is now West Potomac Street. This photo was taken shortly after construction was complete in 1904.

The Brunswick Red Men ready to parade sometime in the early 1900's.

Please don't miss the "Yum-Yum" Dancing Girls at the Red Men's Hall on Friday Night!

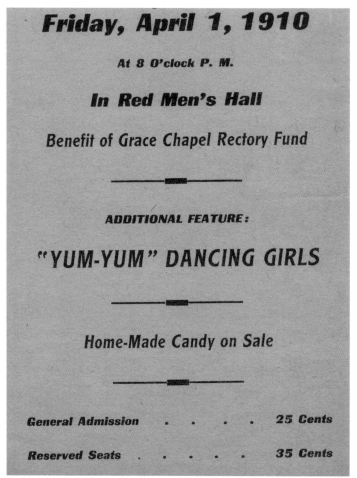

This card was mailed to Red Men members as a reminder of a meeting. This card is from the teens.

Declamation Contest
RED MEN'S HALL

TUESDAY, MARCH 4, 1919

8 O'CLOCK

AUSPICES BRUNSWICK HIGH SCHOOL

Declamation Contest 1919

Declamation Contest

Webster Literary Society of Brunswick High School

Red Men's Hall   April 5, 1924

Declamation Contest 1924

The Brunswick Volunteer Fire Company

"The Fighting Fifth"

An entire book could be dedicated to the Brunswick Fire Company as the information provided by the author is merely a brief introduction to this vital resource that exhibits such pride in volunteerism.

Before the mid 1890's, no real organized effort for fire protection existed except for the formation of bucket brigades.[7] Older generations remember a Howe hand pumper engine, a hook and ladder wagon and several hose reels by the late 1890's.[8] Reel houses were established and there was organization to the operation of each reel house. To offset expenses there was an annual fire company picnic and the reel teams held competitions against each other.[9]

After improvements to the Town water system, the Brunswick Volunteer Fire Department was formed in 1910. The equipment was refurbished and a fire hall was erected on an empty lot opposite of the Imperial Theater.

In January of 1922, a new 750 gallon American LaFrance combined pumper, hose and ladder truck was delivered.[10] In 1930, a Ford-Howe combined pumper, hose and ladder truck was purchased. The entire cost of this engine was completely paid off during the great depression.

In 1928, The Brunswick Mayor and Council built a new fire hall on North Delaware Avenue and turned it over to the Fire Company.[11]

[7]Brunswick:100 Years of Memories, Brunswick History Commission, p138

[8] Brunswick Fire Departments, F.L. Spitzer, Firemen's Convention Program, 1937

[9]ibid 7

[10] Interview with Wade Watson

[11] ibid 8

In 1947, the late Sonny Cannon lead the effort to erect a new Fire Hall on West Potomac Street. The building was paid off in 1953. In 2012, The Brunswick Volunteer Fire Department ceremoniously traveled from the fire hall on West Potomac to their new home at 1500 Volunteer Drive in Brunswick Crossing.

Brunswick Fire Department.

APPLICATION FOR MEMBERSHIP
— IN —

Company No. 3.

BRUNSWICK, MD., _____ 190____

To the Officers and Members of the Brunswick Fire Department :

I hereby present my application for honorary active membership in the above Company and if elected I promise a faithful compliance with the Constitution and the By-Laws of the said Company.

Membership fee of $.......... accompanies this application.

Signed...

Age...............

Recommended by :

....

....

Before joining the Maryland State Fireman's Association 1910 as Company 5 this circa 1900 membership application states they were Company 3.

This badge, circa 1910, is in unused condition and has the original envelope. The badge had a dual purpose. The black side was worn when in mourning and the red side was used for parading and ceremonies.

This Easter Program and Business Men's Directory was published in 1923.

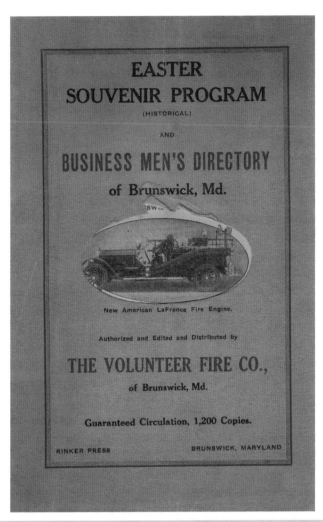

The Ladies of the Fire Company offering flowers and eggs for sale in 1923 in front of the Casino Theater. The Casino Theater was located in the middle area of the J.J. Newberry building. The theater had a balcony.

An ad for an Old–Time July 4th celebration. Fireworks at night.

An Old-Time
Fourth of July Celebration
WITH BIG PARADE—
SPEAKING—EATING—DANCING
AND OTHER AMUSEMENTS.

Wednesday, July 4, 1923

ALL DAY AND NIGHT
BENEFIT OF
VOLUNTEER FIRE COMPANY
Fireworks At Night

PROGRAM

THURSDAY, JULY 15th, 1937.

6:00 P. M.—Registration and Reception of Delegates at Firemen's Hall, N. Delaware Avenue.

8:00 P. M.—Annual Business Session of the Convention—Eagles' Hall, Maryland Avenue and Potomac Street.—Called to order by S. T. Virts, President of the Association. Election of Officers; Selection of Convention town for 1938, etc.

Address of Welcome by Harry R. Mace, Mayor of Brunswick.

Refreshments.

FRIDAY, JULY 16th, 1937.

4:00 P. M.—Parade forms in West End.

5:00 P. M.—Parade moves promptly, passing over the principal streets and disbanding at the City Park.

6:00 to   ?—Supper by Ladies Auxiliary.

6:30 P. M.—Practical demonstration of rescue work by Rescue Team of United's No. 3, of Frederick.

7:00 to   ?—Band Concert.

9:00 P. M.—Awarding of Prizes.

FIREMEN'S CARNIVAL —— CITY PARK

TUESDAY to SATURDAY, JULY 13th to 17th.

BINGO——THE SAMBO GLIDE——RACES——EVERYTHING

FUN —— LAUGHS —— PRIZES

50c—Supper   FRIDAY, JULY 16th   Supper—50c

Fireman's Carnival for 1937.

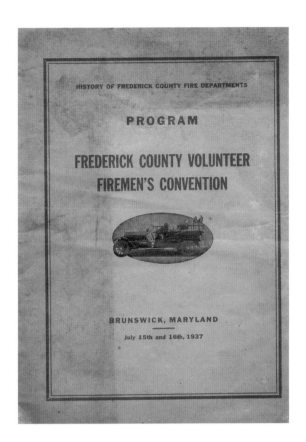

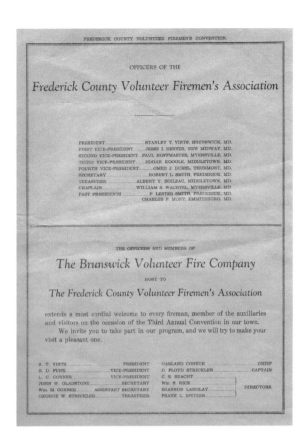

1937 Frederick County Fireman's Convention Program held in Brunswick. The Inside cover page of 1937 program lists the officers of the Brunswick Volunteer Fire Company. In 1937 Stanley Virts was President of the Brunswick Fire Company and the Frederick County Firemen's association.

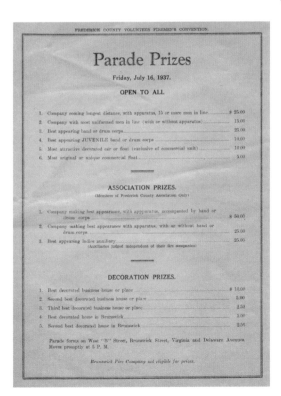

What good is a fireman's convention without a parade? This is the parade prize list for the 1937 fireman's parade. Note the awards for best decorated homes and businesses.

I hope you enjoyed this book.

Coming in 2015:

History In Our Attics:
Photos And Documents of Brunswick, Maryland

Volume II

More Railroad

More Businesses

Gross' Store

More Organizations

Schools

Knoxville

James R. Castle
P.O. Box 8
Brunswick, MD 21716

www.Jamesrcastle.com
www.facebook.com/authorjamesrcastle
Follow me on Twitter @Jamesrcastle
Email:Jamesrcastle@comcast.net

15152453R00058

Made in the USA
San Bernardino, CA
16 September 2014